The Little Book of Listening

Listening games for children in the Early Years Foundation Stage

by Clare Beswick

Illustrations by Julia Oliver

LITTLE BOOKS WITH **BIG** IDEAS

Published 2009 by A&C Black Publishers Limited
36 Soho Square, London W1D 3QY
www.acblack.com

ISBN 978-1-9041-8769-1

First published in the UK by Featherstone Education, 2003

Text © Clare Beswick, 2003
Illustrations © Julia Oliver, 2003
Cover photographs © Shutterstock

A CIP record for this publication is available from the British Library.

Printed in Great Britain by Latimer Trend & Company Limited.

This book is produced using paper that is made from wood grown in
managed, sustainable forests. It is natural, renewable and recyclable.

The logging and manufacturing processes conform to the environmental
regulations of the country of origin.

**To see our full range of titles
visit www.acblack.com**

Contents

Introduction

Listening is a key skill for all of us. Children in the early years need to practise and refine their listening skills to support the development not just of communication and literacy, but as an essential foundation for all their learning.

Children who learn to focus their attention and listen carefully and effectively are well placed to build good relationships with others and make the most of learning opportunities. Moreover, sustaining attentive listening is an important goal within the Foundation Stage.

Good listening skills take time and practice to achieve, and a range of different approaches to developing listening skills is needed to grab and hold the interest of different children and to suit different learning styles.

This book provides plenty of enjoyable, easy to do activities, using materials that are readily to hand in early years settings. It is intended for everyone working with children in the foundation stage, in schools, preschool playgroups, nurseries or in homes. All the activities encourage children's listening skills.

All the activities are:

▶ carefully planned to help children to make progress towards the goals for the Early Years Foundation Stage;
▶ practical, enjoyable and exciting to do;
▶ planned to harness children's natural curiosity;
▶ easily adapted for children at different developmental stages;
▶ ideal for work in small groups or with individual children.

Each activity has a suggested group size, enabling you to match work to the needs and interests of the children in your group. Some of the pages suggest that an activity is suitable for use with individuals – children with special or additional needs, or those who need more practice in listening. These activities are recommended for use by adults (including support assistants) who have responsibility for working with named individuals.

Each activity meets a range of early learning goals, and these appear on the page. The key goals are from the personal, social and emotional development and communication, language and literacy areas of learning:

Personal, Social and Emotional Development

▶ continue to be interested, excited and motivated to learn;

▶ be confident to try new activities, initiate ideas and speak in a familiar group;

▶ maintain attention, concentration and sit quietly when appropriate; consider the consequences of their words and actions for themselves and others.

Communication, Language and Literacy

▶ interact with others, negotiating plans and activities and taking turns in conversations;

▶ enjoy listening to and using spoken and written language, and readily turn to it in their play and learning;

▶ sustain attentive listening, responding to what they have heard by relevant comments, questions or actions;

▶ listen with enjoyment and respond to stories, songs, and other music, rhymes and poems and make up their own stories, rhymes and poems;

▶ extend their vocabulary, exploring the meanings and sounds of new words;

▶ speak clearly and audibly with confidence and control and show awareness for example by their use of conventions such as 'thank you';

▶ use language to imagine and recreate roles and experiences;

- use talk to organise, sequence and clarify thinking, ideas, feelings and events;

- hear and say initial and final sounds in words;

- link letters and sounds, naming and sounding all letters of the alphabet.

Creative Development
- respond in a variety of ways to what they see, hear, smell, touch and feel.

Activities across all six areas of learning are included in this Little Book. These are clearly indicated on each page, along with what you need, what to do and the key words that you and the children will be using.

Several additional activity ideas are listed on each page to either extend or adapt the original activity, or to develop new activities using similar resources, or to achieve the same goals.

The Little Book of Listening makes listening fun and rewarding. Watch the children reap the benefits of being focused and attentive across all areas of learning.

Resources

At the end of this book there is a list of stories which provide good opportunities for children to practise listening. They will be available from good bookshops and libraries. Here is a list of additional resources which readers will also find contain plenty of material to use with children.

'The Little Book of Nursery Rhymes' by Sally Featherstone
ISBN 1-904187-53-6
A selection of traditional and modern rhymes, which give opportunities for listening and for the recognition and development of pattern and rhythm.

'The Little Book of Music' by Anice Paterson & David Wheway
ISBN 1-904187-54-4
Lots of ideas for providing opportunities for children to make and listen to sounds and music.

'The Little Book of Storytelling' by Mary Medlicott
ISBN 1-904187-65-X
All sorts of ideas rhymes and chants, action stories, folk and other tales for children to practise listening.

'The Little Book of Phonics' by Sally Featherstone
ISBN 1-902233-67-0
Links objects and sounds and gives practice in listening to letter sounds and becoming aware of the shapes which make them.

'Clapping Games - Whole Brain Workouts for Lively Children' by Jenny Mosley & Helen Sonnet
Book plus CD (which is available separately) which offer activities which will stimulate both halves of the brain simultaneously, helping to improve its efficiency and raise inteliigence.

'Small Voices, Big Noises' (CD)
A collection of lively songs specially recorded for young children to listen to and to
join in clapping, singing and using simple instruments.

'Carousel' (CD)
40 of the best loved children's songs.

All available from Featherstone Education, PO Box 6350, Lutterworth LE17 6ZA
Phone 0185 888 1212. Fax 0185 888 1360. Email ·info@featherstone.uk.com·

Beat the Drum

Focus: Explore rhythms and practise listening and turn taking

What you need

- wooden and metal spoons
- a large tin or saucepan
- a wooden block or tray
- two or three children

Links with EYFS goals

Personal, Social and Emotional Development
- have a positive approach to new experiences.

Communication, Language and Literacy
- enjoy rhyming and rhythmic activities.

Additional learning outcomes

- To listen and repeat short rhythmic patterns

- To use words to describe sounds and rhythm

- To take turns

Key words

- strong
- gentle
- quick
- slow

What you do

1. Sit on the floor with the children. Give each child a chance to bang the pan or tray and pass it on to the next child, first with a wooden spoon, then with a metal one.

2. Choose metal or wooden spoons. Beat out a two or three beat rhythm on the pan or tray. Go round the group, taking turns to copy the sound and the rhythm.

3. Talk about the number of beats and the strength of each beat ('strong' or 'gentle').

4. Encourage the children to describe the sounds and try to make new sounds to pass round the group.

5. Now try with the other sort of spoons, or use the wooden block or tray.

More ideas...

▶ Add scraping sounds to the patterns by rubbing the spoons across the tray or pan.

▶ Look out for tapes of drumming music to inspire the children.

▶ Sing "Incy Wincey Spider" and beat the drum each time you sing the word "Incy".

▶ Give each child a drum and sing "The children play with one drum, one drum, one drum, this fine day" to the tune of "Peter Hammers with one Hammer". (This Little Puffin)

Activity suitable for:

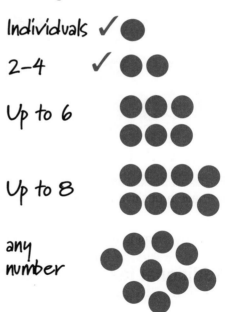

Individuals ✓

2-4 ✓

Up to 6

Up to 8

any number

Listen!

Focus: **Listen hard for hidden sounds**

What you need

- ▶ a clock with a loud tick
- ▶ a kitchen timer
- ▶ a wind up musical toy
- ▶ a music box

Links with EYFS goals

Personal, Social and Emotional Development
- ▶ display high levels of involvement in an activity.

Communication, Language and Literacy
- ▶ sustain attentive listening.

Problem Solving, Reasoning and Numeracy
- ▶ observe and use positional language.

Additional learning outcomes

- – To listen and repeat short rhythmic patterns

- – To use words to describe sounds and rhythm

- – To take turns

Key words

- ▶ close
- ▶ far
- ▶ louder
- ▶ quieter
- ▶ near
- ▶ muffled/clear

What you do

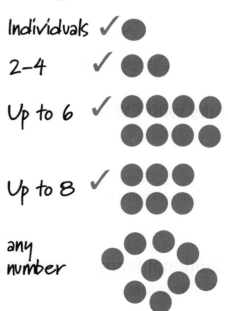

1. Gather the children in a group and explain the game.

2. Ask the children to close their eyes while you hide one of the sound makers.

3. Return to the group and listen with them. Talk about what you can hear. Help them guess what is making the sound.

4. Now try again with a different sound maker.

5. Choose a child to find the object and check if you were right.

6. Play again, this time with one of the children hiding a sound maker.

7. Make the game more difficult by hiding two or three sound makers in different places.

8. Describe one of the sounds and try to find each one in turn.

More ideas...

▶ Find three boxes. Hide the clock in one box and let the children guess which one it is in.

▶ Bury a kitchen timer in dry sand. Let each child guess where it is and stick a lolly stick in the sand. The nearest one buries the timer again.

▶ Play "I hear with my little ear, something that sounds like... ".

▶ Make a tape of your sound makers and play a matching game with the objects or pictures/photos of them.

Activity suitable for:

Individuals ✓ ●

2-4 ✓ ● ●

Up to 6 ✓ ● ● ● ●
● ● ● ●

Up to 8 ✓ ● ● ●
● ● ●

any
number ● ● ●
● ● ●
● ● ●

Hide and Seek

Focus: A new twist on a traditional game for finding and discriminating between sounds

What you need

- ▶ space and hiding places outside
- ▶ a sound maker for each child, e.g. tambourine, clicker, bells, sticks, spoons, plastic box, scrunchy paper or foil.

I will need

Links with EYFS goals

Personal, Social and Emotional Development
- ▶ work as part of a group, taking turns and sharing fairly.

Communication, Language and Literacy.
- ▶ use a widening range of words.

Creative Development
- ▶ explore and learn how sounds can be changed.

Additional learning outcomes

- – To use describing words
- – To locate hidden sounds
- – To follow simple rules for a game

Key words
- ▶ click
- ▶ tinkle
- ▶ tap
- ▶ crunch
- ▶ crinkle
- ▶ jingle

What you do

1. Explain the special game of hide and seek to the children.

2. Invite one child to be the first seeker.

3. Give all the other children a sound maker and then, while the seeker has their eyes covered, encourage the other children to tip-toe away to hide.

4. Count to ten slowly with the seeker and then help the seeker to find the other children one by one. Begin by saying 'Let's find a tapping sound,' so that all the children with tapping sound makers tap away for the seeker to locate them. When the child has found all the tappers, they must look for the jinglers, and so on.

5. When everyone has been found, choose another seeker.

More ideas...

▶ Gently blindfold the seeker and ask the other children sit on the floor with their sound makers. Point to one of the children, who makes their sound. When the seeker locates one of the sounds, they guess the sound maker or describe the sound.

▶ Sing "I am the Music Man" outside using natural sound makers such as rustling leaves, tapping twigs, creaking branches, bicycle bells. Sing "I can play on the hard dry sticks; the wooden fence; the metal bike..." etc.

Activity suitable for:

Individuals

2-4

Up to 6

Up to 8 ✓

any number

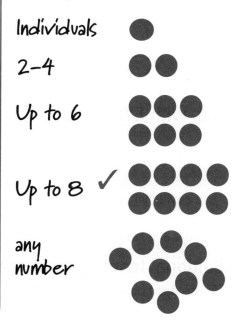

13

Ready Steady Go!

Focus: Get active with this lively listening and memory game

What you need

I will need

- ► a large space, inside or in the garden
- ► three different sound makers, e.g. a shaker, bells, wooden blocks, tambourine

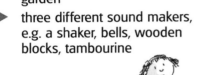

Links with EYFS goals

Communication, Language and Literacy
- ► Sustain attentive listening.

Physical Development
- ► Show respect for other children's personal space; move with control and co-ordination.

Additional learning outcomes

- – To listen whilst being active

- – To recall the sounds and actions

- – To negotiate space and take part in a game with others

Key words
- ► stop/go
- ► fast/slow
- ► space
- ► stretch
- ► listen
- ► move/still

What you do

1. Explain the game, emphasising that it is about 'good listening'.

2. First they need to listen to how they should move – walking, crawling, rolling, running, jumping and so on.

3. When they hear one sound (e.g. the bells), they move. When they hear the second sound (e.g. the shaker) they stop.

4. Play several times, sometimes playing the stopping or starting sound twice, until they can follow, then try playing the sound behind a chair or in a box, so they can't see which instrument you are using.

5. To make the game more difficult, add a third sound (e.g. a wood block) to indicate a third movement. Now play a pattern to follow – e.g. walk, stop, run, stop, run, stop, walk.

More ideas...

▶ Give each sound a location. The children run to that area when they hear that sound, e.g. over by the gate when they hear the shaker.

▶ Read The Very Hungry Caterpillar. Talk about how a caterpillar hatches from an egg, grows slowly builds a cocoon and emerges as a butterfly. Choose instruments for each stage. Ask the children to curl up as tiny eggs and to listen for when the egg hatches. Continue the story with different sounds.

Activity suitable for:

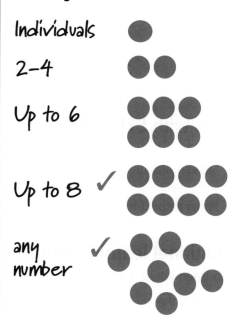

Individuals

2-4

Up to 6

Up to 8 ✓

any number ✓

Kitchen Sounds

Focus: Listening to and identifying familiar sounds

What you need

- ▶ dried pasta, a bowl and a spoon
- ▶ a jug of water and a bowl
- ▶ pots, pans and cutlery
- ▶ a box of cereal, a clock and keys

I will need

Links with EYFS goals

Communication, Language and Literacy
- ▶ use vocabulary focused on familiar objects and people.

Knowledge and Understanding of the World
- ▶ Investigate objects by using all their senses, as appropriate.

Additional learning outcomes

- – To listen to and identify familiar sounds
- – To recall a sequence of sounds
- – To speak clearly and take turns

Key words

- ▶ ping
- ▶ whirr
- ▶ rattle
- ▶ shake
- ▶ bang
- ▶ crash

What you do

1. You could set up this activity in your home corner.

2. Sit the children with their backs to you, and explain that you are going to make some kitchen sounds to guess.

3. Make different sounds for the children to listen to, describe and identify – clanking the cutlery, clock ticking, rattling keys, pouring cereal from the box, opening and closing the cupboard door, rattling the pans and so on.

4. Let some of the children have a turn at making the sounds.

5. Now talk about the other sounds they hear in the kitchen – the microwave pinging, doors slamming or a liquidiser whirring.

6. To make the game more difficult, try a series of less usual sounds, such as pouring cereal, adding milk or sprinkling sugar.

More ideas...

▶ Look at pictures of kitchen equipment in a catalogue or magazine and talk about the sounds they make.

▶ Use sounds that they might hear in the bathroom, such as a tap running, teeth being brushed, hands being washed, water dripping and so on.

▶ Play a listening and memory game like " I went to the shops and bought...". Begin with "In my house I heard the TV". The next child says, "In my house I heard the TV and the dog barking", etc.

Activity suitable for:

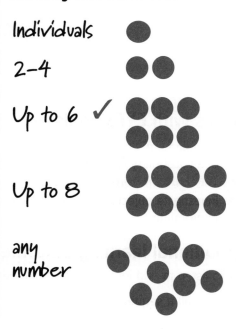

Individuals

2-4

Up to 6 ✓

Up to 8

any number

Red, yellow, blue and green

Focus: Have rainbow fun with this listening skills parachute game

What you need

- ▶ a parachute or large sheet
- ▶ balloons – red, blue, yellow and green

I will need

Links with EYFS goals

Personal, Social and Emotional Development
- ▶ form good relationships with peers.

Communication, Language and Literacy
- ▶ listen to others in small groups.

Problem Solving, Reasoning and Numeracy
- ▶ count up to three objects, saying one number name for each item.

Additional learning outcomes

- – To recognise colours
- – To count up to three objects
- – To follow simple instructions
- – To understand on and under

N.B. Collect any burst balloons, as they are a choking hazard!

Key words

- ▶ colours and numbers
- ▶ high/low
- ▶ fast/slow
- ▶ on/under
- ▶ up/down

What you do

1. Spread the sheet or parachute out on the floor and ask the children to sit around the edge. Grab the edges of the parachute and practice wafting the sheet up and down.

2. Now ask the children in turn to follow your instructions to:
   ▶ put a red balloon on the parachute, or two red balloons under the parachute, or one green balloon under the parachute, or perhaps a red and a yellow balloon.

3. Waft the parachute gently up and down, then lay it on the floor, and ask children to collect balloons according to your instructions – e.g. get the red balloon under the parachute; or the two green balloons from on top of the parachute.

4. Play the game again till everyone has had a turn.

More ideas...

▶ Place all the balloons under the parachute and take turns to collect balloons of a named colour.

▶ Give the children turns at giving the instructions of the balloons to be collected – this helps with listening to each other as well as to you! Try whispering or singing instructions.

▶ Add some beanbags or soft balls. Encourage the children to listen carefully to the number of beanbags, balls or balloons they need to collect from under or on the parachute.

Activity suitable for:

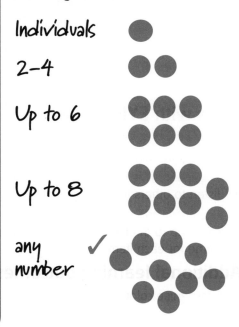

Individuals

2-4

Up to 6

Up to 8

any number ✓

19

Fly That Plane!

Focus: Bring together physical skills and listening with some target play

What you need

- ▶ paper and pens
- ▶ hoops of several colours
- ▶ masking or duct tape
- ▶ chalk

I will need

Links with EYFS goals

Communication, Language and Literacy
- ▶ engage in activities requiring hand-eye co-ordination.

Physical Development
- ▶ use increasing control over objects, by pushing, patting or throwing.

Additional learning outcomes

- – To fold paper carefully
- – To imitate actions and listen to instructions
- – To throw towards a target
- – To practice mark-making

Key words

- ▶ near
- ▶ far
- ▶ high
- ▶ low
- ▶ fold
- ▶ wing

What you do

1. Help the children to make simple paper aeroplanes. Practice accurate folding. Use the pens to add windows, maybe a pilot and the name or number of the plane.

2. Tape the hoops to the floor to prevent them sliding when stepped on.

3. Explain how to play the game. The children must wait till the word 'Go' before throwing their plane towards the hoop you name.

4. Now ask each child to throw a plane towards a named hoop – e.g. the yellow hoop. Encourage them to listen carefully and release their plane on the word 'GO' of 'Ready, steady, go.'

More ideas...

▶ Whisper or sing the instructions.

▶ Give the hoops numbers or letters instead of identifying them by colour.

▶ Put a set of bells in one hoop, a shaker in another. Play a matching instrument and encourage the children to throw their plane to the hoop with the instrument that makes the same sound.

▶ Hang the hoops from branches, doorways and see if they can launch the plane through the hoop.

Activity suitable for:

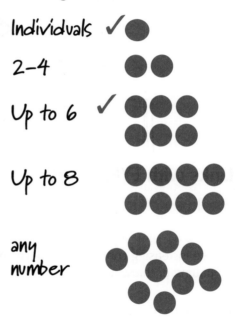

Individuals ✓

2-4

Up to 6 ✓

Up to 8

any number

Animal Fun

Focus: **Get creative with some big movements and jungle fun**

What you need

- a shaker, drum, clacker or other sound makers
- a big space, with a clean floor, where children can move freely

Links with EYFS goals

Communication, Language and Literacy
- to respond to simple instructions.

Physical Development
- move in a range of ways; negotiate space successfully.

Creative Development
- express and communicate ideas.

Additional learning outcomes

- To listen and match sounds to actions
- To follow simple rules
- To use large and small movements
- To make good use of available space

Key words

- fast/slow
- heavy
- nimble
- stampede
- amble
- slither

What you do

1. Talk to the children about different wild animals. Think about the way they move and try out some of the actions. Explain that you are going to play a listening game.

2. Choose three animals to be represented by your chosen sounds, perhaps a hissing snake slithering along the ground for the shaker, an elephant plodding along for the drum and maybe an antelope skipping around for the clacker. Try to use the children's own ideas.

3. Ask the children to curl up on the floor and listen for the sounds. When they hear each sound they can move around like that animal. Try out different ways of moving and encourage the children to imitate each other.

More ideas...

▶ Vary the pace of the drumbeat and the shaker, so that maybe a fast beat for the elephants stampeding and a very slow beat for a gentle plodding amble through the jungle.

▶ Play "I hear with my little ear, something that sounds like... ".

▶ Turn each child into a jungle explorer. When they hear the shaker they are on a boat going along a river. Shake it faster as you come to the rapids.
Beat the drum slowly as they climb out of the boat and up the bank.

Activity suitable for:

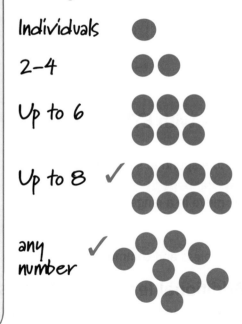

Individuals

2-4

Up to 6

Up to 8 ✓

any number ✓

First Sounds

Focus: Practice listening for and recognising initial letter sounds

What you need

▶ space on the carpet
▶ a basket of objects with initial letter sounds matching the initials of the children playing (up to three of each)

I will need

Links with EYFS goals

Personal, Social and Emotional Development
▶ be confident to try new activities, initiate ideas and speak in a familiar group.

Communication, Language and Literacy
▶ Hear and say initial and final sounds.

Additional learning outcomes

– Additional learning intentions

– To take turns

– To identify and match initial letter sounds

Key words

▶ letter sounds
▶ first
▶ sound
▶ beginning
▶ end

What you do

1. Take it in turns to choose any item from the basket to explore. Talk about what the object is used for, what it is made of and so on.

2. Think about the name of the object that is the first sound you can hear.

3. Match this up to the name of a child in the group.

4. Give the object to the child and they can then choose the next object to talk about.

5. Continue until the basket is empty.

6. Make the game more difficult by listening for final sounds as well, or by having a mixture of objects with different initial letters in the basket.

More ideas...

▶ Use a variety of objects all linked to a theme, such as clothes or transport, and sort these out by initial letter sound.

▶ Have a tray of objects with the same initial sound, such as bus, ball, bat, book and one more with a different sound, perhaps a car. Play a game of odd one out.

▶ Give each child a basket or shoebox and attach a label with a letter. Ask them to collect objects from around the room that begin with that letter.

Activity suitable for:

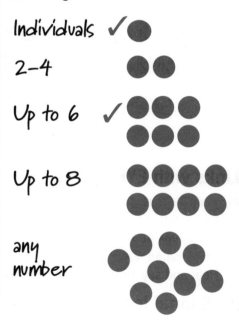

Individuals ✓

2-4

Up to 6 ✓

Up to 8

any number

Quiz Time

Focus: Make the most of a simple cassette recorder for some listening fun

What you need

- a cassette recorder
- a blank tape
- a box or basket of dressing up clothes

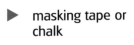

- masking tape or chalk

I will need

Links with EYFS goals

Communication, Language and Literacy

- maintain attention, concentrate and sit quietly when appropriate; dress and undress independently.
- sustain attentive listening.

Additional learning outcomes

- To listen to and respond to instructions
- To be part of a team
- To practice dressing, managing simple fasteners independently

Key words

- names of clothes
- body part names
- listen
- team
- collect

What you do

1. Record a tape of instructions for each team in turn, such as "Red team, find a hat for each person," "Blue team choose a pair of shoes each." The tape should have enough instructions for all the clothes in the box!

2. Mark an area for each team with tape or chalk, and put the dressing up box between the two teams.

3. Make two teams of children (younger children might need coloured stickers or wrist bands to help them remember!)

4. Play the tape and help them follow their team's instructions.

5. Now race to put on all the clothes.

6. Rewind the tape and play it again as they follow the instructions to take the clothes off again.

More ideas...

▶ Play this game with everyday items they can easily gather from around the room – an apron, book and so on.

▶ Make a recording of the children's names arranged randomly and repeated several times. Play a game that when they hear their name on the tape they have to stand up, turn round and sit down again.

▶ Invite the children to record their favourite nursery rhymes. Play back the tape asking the other children to guess who is singing.

Activity suitable for:

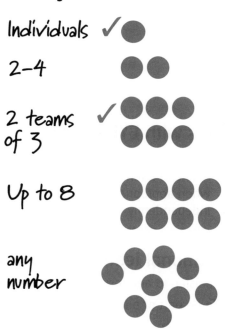

Individuals ✓

2-4

2 teams of 3 ✓

Up to 8

any number

A Treasure Hunt of Sounds

Focus: **A great listening game for outside**

What you need

- ▶ a big sheet of paper, clipboards or whiteboards
- ▶ pens
- ▶ a camera (not essential)

Links with EYFS goals

Personal, Social and Emotional Development
- ▶ adapt their behaviour to events and changes in routine.

Communication, Language and Literacy
- ▶ ascribe meaning to marks; use writing as a means of recording.

Additional learning outcomes

- – To listen for and identify sounds
- – To discriminate between sounds
- – To use pictures and words to convey information

Key words

- ▶ loud/quiet
- ▶ coming/going away
- ▶ soft
- ▶ squeaking
- ▶ rustling
- ▶ clanking

What you do

1. Gather the children in a group and explain the game.

2. Ask them to listen very carefully for sounds in the room, then ask them what sort of sounds they might hear outside.

3. Make picture/word lists of all the sounds they suggest. The children could help, or make their own on white boards or clip boards.

4. Go out together and see if you can find each of the sounds in turn. If you hear other sounds, add them to your lists.

5. Use a wide range of describing words to talk about the sounds you hear. Ask the children to listen for sounds that change – birdsong, footsteps, planes, or perhaps traffic as it gets closer.

More ideas...

▶ Sing "The plane in the sky goes vroom, vroom, vroom...." to 'The Wheels on the Bus".

▶ Ask a parent to bring a very young baby into your setting. Listen carefully with the children to the different sounds the baby makes. What is the baby telling us with the different sounds? Make a tape to listen to later, perhaps with photos.

▶ Talk to the children about different ways you can use your voice – singing, whispering and humming, etc.

Activity suitable for:

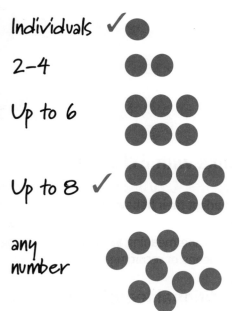

Individuals ✓

2-4

Up to 6

Up to 8 ✓

any number

What's That?

Focus: Practice listening to descriptions

What you need

▶ 10 or 12 everyday objects such as keys, glasses, an egg whisk, a sponge, shampoo, a trowel, a mobile phone, a spoon or a mug

Links with EYFS goals

Personal, Social and Emotional Development
▶ work as part of a group.

Communication, Language and Literacy
▶ extend their vocabulary, exploring meanings and sounds of new words.

Knowledge and Understanding of the world
▶ talk about what is happening.

Additional learning outcomes

– To take turns
– To identify and match initial letter sounds

Key words
▶ heavy/light
▶ metal
▶ plastic
▶ wood
▶ glass
▶ hard

What you do

1. Gather the children in a group on the carpet, and spread the objects on the floor. Look at each one and talk about what they are, and what they are called.

2. Ask the children to cover their eyes and listen very carefully. Describe one of the objects by their use, such as "Something you use in the bathroom when you get washed".

3. Help the children to name the object without looking. Prompt with simple open questions. Let the children open their eyes and look at the objects again to check.

4. Make the game harder with more complex and intricate objects such as a postcard, measuring jug, ruler and so on. Make it easier by having just a few very familiar objects.

More ideas...

▶ Play this game with photographs or pictures.

▶ Let the children take it in turns to describe how one of the objects is used. Help the other children to guess which object this is.

▶ Think about sounds that you can hear at home. Mime the actions or function of the sound maker, and add the sounds it makes, or how it is used. Can the children guess which sound and sound maker you are thinking of?

Activity suitable for:

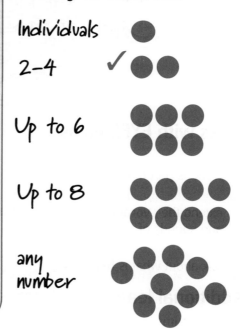

Individuals

2–4 ✓

Up to 6

Up to 8

any number

Hat, Cat, Bat!

Focus: Enjoy sharing some simple rhymes to inspire your own rhyming strings

What you need

▶ a rhyming book such as "Mr Brown Can Moo, Can You?" or "Pass the Jam Jim"

For a book list see page 64

Links with EYFS goals

Personal, Social and Emotional Development
▶ be confident to try new activities.

Communication, Language and Literacy
▶ show awareness of rhyme and alliteration; recognise rhyme in words; continue a rhyming string.

Additional learning outcomes

– To listen carefully

– To find rhyming words

– To continue a string of rhyming words

Key words

▶ same/different

▶ rhyme/rhyming

▶ sound

▶ first sound

▶ last sound

▶ end

What you do

1. Read the rhyming story book.

2. Talk about some of the words and phrases used. Listen for rhyming words. Say some of these in a sing-song pattern.

3. Choose one of the words and ask the children to suggest words that rhyme. Make up nonsense words and phrases.

4. Try passing a word around the group. Start with a simple words, such as "hat". Then ask the children to taking turns to add another word that rhymes, such as "cat hat" and so on. You could have a rhyming hat to pass round the group!

5. Encourage the children to listen carefully to the words and sounds and also to listen carefully to each other, avoiding interruptions.

More ideas...

▶ Link the game to your theme or topic (such as animals). Ask the first child to choose an animal and then count how many rhyming words you can find for that animal name.

▶ Play "Odd One Out" with a box of objects or pictures of objects that rhyme, with one extra object that does not rhyme.

▶ Sing or make up simple rhythmic songs with strong rhymes.

'The Little Book of Nursery Rhymes' has many favourites.

Activity suitable for:

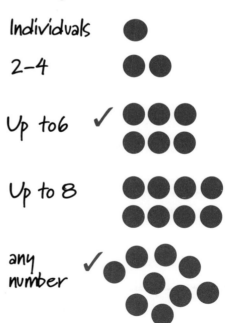

Individuals ●

2–4 ●●

Up to 6 ✓ ●●● ●●●

Up to 8 ●●●● ●●●●

any number ✓ ●●● ●●● ●●●●

Thread a Sound

Focus: Find out about different sounds and sound makers

What you need

▶ scissors
▶ catalogues and junk mail
▶ a hole punch
▶ ribbon or string

I will need

Links with EYFS goals

Communication, Language and Literacy
▶ interact with others, negotiating plans and activities.
Knowledge and Understanding of the World
▶ look closely at similarities and differences, patterns and change

Additional learning outcomes

– To identify and sort different sounds and sound makers
– To use scissors and thread accurately

Key words

▶ buzz/ring
▶ loud/soft
▶ shrill
▶ whizz/whirr
▶ click/clack
▶ hum/tick

What you do

1. Look through the pictures together. Look for things that make sounds or noises.

2. Talk about the different sounds made by different objects, people, animals and machine – a telephone ringing, a drill whirring, a shoe tapping, a watch ticking, a bird singing.

3. Encourage the children to use a wide variety of describing words for the different sounds that the objects make.

4. Help the children to cut out each of the items and then to make a hole in the picture with the hole-punch.

5. Thread all the objects that make loud noises onto one ribbon, all the quiet sounds on another, all the tapping and clicking noises on another ribbon, all the animal sounds on another.

More ideas...

▶ Find pictures of all the machines in your setting that make a noise, then pictures of machines at home. Talk about the different types of sounds, such as the ringing of the doorbell, the clicking of the computer keyboard, the pinging of the microwave.

▶ Look at pictures of different clocks. Can you guess what they might sound like? Listen to a watch and an alarm clock. Can you hear the different ticks?

▶ Accompany "Hickory Dickory Dock" with ticks and tocks.

Activity suitable for:

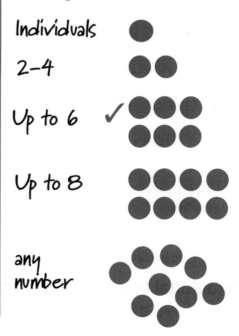

Individuals

2–4

Up to 6 ✓

Up to 8

any number

Make and Change

Focus: Experiment with making and changing sounds

What you need

- boxes, tins and containers
- different sorts of paper
- bubble wrap, sticks and spoons
- coins, pasta or rice

I will need

Links with EYFS goals

Personal, Social and Emotional Development
- display high levels of involvement.

Communication, Language and Literacy
- use talk to connect ideas, explain anticipate what might happen next.

Knowledge and Understanding of the World
- investigate pattern and change.

Additional learning outcomes

- To listen to and describe sounds
- To investigate and try out their own ideas
- To play alongside others

Key words

- different
- jingle, clunk, clatter
- ring, tinkle, click
- louder/softer
- higher/lower
- solid/hollow

What you do

1. Work alongside the children to make different types of musical instruments. Encourage them to experiment with the different types of sounds they can make.

2. Arrange for this activity to be available to the children for several consecutive sessions so that the children can go back to it frequently to develop their ideas and theories.

3. Use a wide range of describing words. Talk about what their instrument sounds like. Ask open questions and allow plenty of time for talk, uninterrupted play and investigation.

4. Put objects in containers and listen to the sounds they make. Use different materials to make drums and shakers.

5. Change and develop the instruments and listen to the change.

More ideas...

▶ Play some percussion music – such as Rhythm song by Evelyn Glennie, classical guitar music, drumming, pop, world music or big band music.

▶ Ask parents to bring in instruments and show the children how they can make and change the sounds. Other parents or staff could bring in their favourite music CD or tape to share with the children. Have a concert!

▶ Visit your local library for music tapes and books. Look out for pictures of musical instruments.

Activity suitable for:

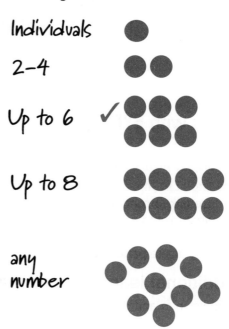

Individuals

2–4

Up to 6 ✓

Up to 8

any number

Hands and Feet

Focus: Use hands and feet to make and imitate different sounds

What you need

- hand and foot print cards
- clothing items for hands and feet (e.g. socks, shoes, gloves, leg warmers, arm bands, flippers and rubber gloves)

Links with EYFS goals

Personal, Social and Emotional Development
- have a positive approach to new experiences.

Communication, Language and Literacy
- distinguish one sound from another. what might happen next.

Creative Development
- enjoy dancing and ring games.

Additional learning outcomes

- To imitate sounds and actions
- To work as part of a group

Key words
- clap
- tap
- stamp
- fast/slow
- loud/soft
- short/long

What you do

1. Gather the children in a circle and explain the game.

2. Ask the children to choose a card (either a hand or a foot).

3. All the children who have chosen a handprint stand up.

4. Use the tune of "Here We go Round the Mulberry bush" and begin by singing "This is the way we clap hands, clap our hands, clap our hands this is the way we clap our hands on a cold and frosty morning". Sing several verses (clap, flick, wave, wiggle, etc.). As they make each sound the children sitting in the circle should sing along and copy.

5. Play again with the children holding the footprints. Try to make lots of different sounds – stamp, jump, hop, tiptoe.

6. Now choose an item of clothing and use it to make a sound.

More ideas...

▶ Play "Pass the Sound". Make a sound with your face, perhaps a sniff, a blow, whistle, hum, huff, sucking sound. Pass the sound around the group, with each child in turn copying the child next to them.

▶ Sing "Everybody do this, do this, do this, everybody do this just like me." Make a range of different actions and sounds for the children to imitate – tapping elbows together, slapping knees together gently, bouncing bottoms on the floor.

Activity suitable for:

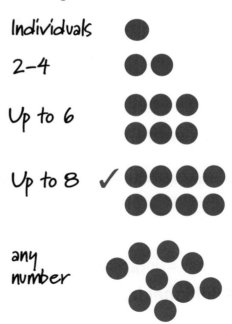

Individuals

2–4

Up to 6

Up to 8 ✓

any number

Crunch, Scrunch, Scrape

Focus: Get creative with some 'sounds messy' play

What you need

- gravel, pebbles and dry sand
- tin lidsand plastic trays
- tractors, dumpers and diggers
- sand or cement mixing tray

Links with EYFS goals

Communication, Language and Literacy
- use a widening range of words to explore and experiment with sounds, words and text.

Knowledge and Understanding of the World
- examine and find out about objects.

Additional learning outcomes

– To find, use and talk about words that describe sounds

– To investigate sounds and how they can change

Key words
- tyres/wheels/engine
- scrunch
- crackle
- crunch
- whirr
- power

What you do

1. Read "Dazzling Diggers" or another construction focused story.

2. Set up a messy play area with trays and tin lids of gravel and pebbles. Keep the sand in the sand tray shallow and dry so that the wheels can be heard crunching and scrunching.

3. Play alongside the children talking about the different sounds the machines make rolling over the different surfaces. Ask open questions and make comments on what you can see.

4. Look at the book again, find some words used to describe the digger noises and see if you can make those noises in the sand tray, or with the gravel and pebbles. Make the same or different noises with the diggers.

More ideas...

► Try larger cars and trucks outside on different surfaces. Listen to and talk about the different sounds.

► Ride bikes on grass and through puddles. Talk about the different sounds you can hear.

► Go out for a walk and listen to the traffic noises. Draw pictures of the different vehicles. Add captions to describe the sounds you can hear. Talk about engines working to go up hill, working hard to pull heavy loads.

Activity suitable for:

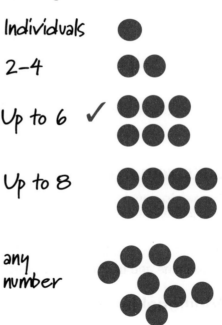

Individuals

2–4

Up to 6 ✓

Up to 8

any number

Splish, Splosh, Drip, Drop

Focus: Listening and making sounds in water fun

What you need

- colanders, droppers and tubes
- bottles, containers and hoses
- water wheels, funnels and lids

- sponges, scoops and cups

Links with EYFS goals

Personal, Social and Emotional Development
- work as part of a group taking turns and sharing fairly.

Knowledge and Understanding of the World
- investigate objects and materials, living things and events they observe.

Additional learning outcomes

- To find, use and talk about words that describe sounds
- To investigate sounds and how they can change

Key words
- splish, splosh, splat
- drip, dribble
- gush, pour
- squeeze
- sponge
- absorb

What you do

1. Talk about all the different water sounds you might hear.

2. Play alongside the children in the water tray and try to make lots of different sounds with the water. Try pouring or dripping water onto the tin lids or the sponges. How do the sounds change?

3. Talk about rain – the pitter patter on the glass, drips from the gutter, splashing from drainpipes, whooshing as the bus goes through a puddle, the drumming of heavy rain on a roof. Talk about water sounds at bath time or in the kitchen.

4. Make a list of all the words that describe the sounds you have made in the water. Display this list next to the water tray with the objects you used to make the sounds.

More ideas...

▶ Fill some watering cans and see how the water sounds when poured with and then without the nozzle. Try it on different surfaces.

▶ Fill the water tray with warm water and lots of different sponges. Experiment with the different sounds you can make.

▶ Put a layer of pebbles at the bottom of a washing up bowl. Add a water wheel. Listen to the sounds of the water falling on the pebbles from the water wheel.

Activity suitable for:

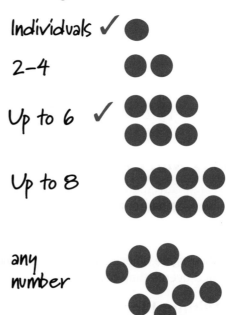

Individuals ✓ ●

2–4 ● ●

Up to 6 ✓ ● ● ● / ● ● ●

Up to 8 ● ● ● ● / ● ● ● ●

any number ● ● ● ● ● ● ● ● ● ●

Clapping and Tapping

Focus: Listen carefully to and copy familiar sound patterns and rhythms

What you need

▶ an everyday object for each child to tap a rhythm – a book, pan, plastic bowl, waste paper bin, shoe box, sticks, bells

I will need

Links with EYFS goals

Personal, Social and Emotional Development
▶ be confident to try new activities; maintain attention, sit quietly and concentrate when appropriate.

Communication, Language and Literacy
▶ to enjoy rhyming/rhythmic activities.

Additional learning outcomes

– To distinguish between sounds

– To imitate patterns of sound

– To take part in a game

Key words

▶ finger tips

▶ loud/soft

▶ click

▶ clap

▶ tap

▶ rub

What you do

1. Begin by singing hello to each child in turn and tapping the syllables of their name out, such as "Hello Lucy, hello Lucy, hello, hello, hello". Each "Hello" would need two taps and then each "Lucy" a long tap and a short tap.

2. Invite each child to sing or tap back hello to you. When the children have the idea, encourage them to join in with the singing and the tapping.

3. Now tap out the syllables of one of the children's name. See if they can guess who's name it is.

4. Play again clapping the names rather than tapping. Encourage the children to take a turn.

5. Try some sequences of taps, to be answered by the children.

More ideas...

▶ Tap or clap out the first line of a very familiar nursery rhyme. Can the children guess what it is going to be? Tap out the whole nursery rhyme together.

▶ Practice clapping loudly and then softly. Make a short pattern of loud and soft claps for the children to copy.

▶ Try other body parts for tapping and clapping such as feet, knees or elbows. How does the sound change?

Activity suitable for:

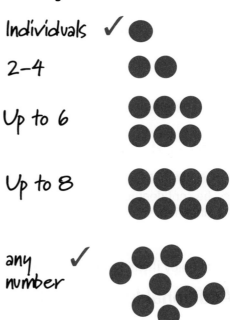

Individuals ✓

2-4

Up to 6

Up to 8

any number ✓

What Did Simon Say?

Focus: **A themed variation on an old favourite**

What you need

- ▶ a clock with a loud tick
- ▶ a kitchen timer
- ▶ a wind up musical toy
- ▶ a music box

Links with EYFS goals

Communication, Language and Literacy
- ▶ sustain attentive listening, responding to what they have heard with relevant comments, actions.

Physical Development
- ▶ move with confidence, imagination.

Additional learning outcomes

- – To follow simple rules of a game
- – To listen carefully
- – To imitate actions

Key words

- ▶ stop
- ▶ go
- ▶ listen, think, act
- ▶ instructions
- ▶ follow

What you do

1. Decide on a theme for your 'Simon Says' game. Choose either an area of learning or a topic that you might be working on such the seaside, colours or people who help us. For **Physical Development** you could play a game of 'Simon Says' focusing on big movements such as wriggling, rolling, stretching, striding, jumping, curling, waving. For a game focused on small movements suggest tapping, shaking, winking.

   For **Personal, Social and Emotional Development** suggest actions where the children might work together, e.g. by holding hands, or skipping together.

   For **Communication, Language and Literacy** pretend to read a book, stand on one leg if your name begins with "S" or write shapes or letters in the air.

   For **Problem Solving, Reasoning and Numeracy** use shapes, numbers or colours to follow.

More ideas...

▶ Play a game of Simon says with all the children sitting in a circle. Have three or four everyday objects in the middle of the circle and say " Simon says pass teddy round". Pass teddy from one to another, and then perhaps say "Simon says go the other way".

Change the direction, add and take away objects to be passed around, all the time making some requests with Simon says and other requests without, which are ignored.

Activity suitable for:

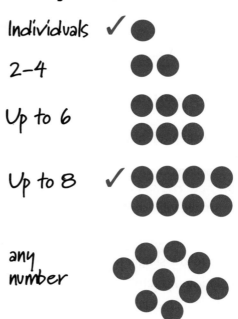

Individuals ✓

2-4

Up to 6

Up to 8 ✓

any number

Letters and Sounds

Focus: Listen for the first sounds in words and make some matching play dough letters

What you need

- playdough
- about six everyday objects
  e.g. apron, book, banana,
  pencil and cup.
- small white
  boards or card and
  pens

Links with EYFS goals

Communication, Language and Literacy
- hear and say initial sounds in words; link
  sounds to letters, naming and sounding the
  letters of the alphabet.

Additional learning outcomes

- To name and hear the initial sound of everyday
  object words
- To match letter shapes

Key words
- first
- sound
- letter
- word
- object

What you do

1. Choose one of the everyday objects. Talk about the object and how it is used. Identify the initial sound in the word.

2. Write the initial letter on a white board.

3. Play alongside the children rolling balls of dough with the palm of your hand to make long sausage shapes of dough.

4. Describe one sound and try to find each one in turn. Play alongside the children as they form their dough to make the initial letter.

5. Help each child to check that their play dough letter matches the letter on the card.

6. As you play, talk about other objects with the same initial letter sound. Encourage the children to join in with the words.

More ideas...

▶ Describe an object that you can see and ask the children to listen carefully to its description and then name the object.

▶ Play this game outside writing letters with a stick dipped in a puddle or a decorator's brush and water.

▶ Write in very wet sand using fingers or small tools such as lolly sticks or dough tools.

▶ Identify the end sound of words and then make play dough letters to match.

Activity suitable for:

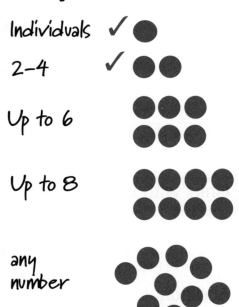

Individuals ✓ ●

2–4 ✓ ● ●

Up to 6 ● ● ● / ● ● ●

Up to 8 ● ● ● ● / ● ● ● ●

any number ● ● ● / ● ● ● ● / ● ● ●

Number Fun

Focus: Try this listening game under a parachute or big sheet

What you need

▶ a parachute or light sheet
▶ a box of toy cars

I will need

Links with EYFS goals

Personal, Social and Emotional Development
▶ work as part of a group or class.

Problem Solving, Reasoning and Numeracy
▶ count reliably up to 10

Physical Development
▶ show respect for other children's personal space

Additional learning outcomes

– To listen for and act on a sound
– To recognise colours
– To stretch up high, bend down low and sit down
  at the same time as the group

Key words

▶ up/down
▶ stop/start
▶ tall, taller
▶ long, longer
▶ traffic

What you do

1. Put the box of cars on the floor and spread the parachute or sheet out on the floor over the box. Sit round the edge.

2. Lift the parachute up together as high as you can reach while still sitting. Pull the parachute down behind you and sit on the edges so that you have made a tent. The box of cars will be in the middle of your tent.

3. Explain that you are going to make a huge traffic jam going right around the inside of the parachute.

4. Ask each child in turn to collect cars from the box – three cars, or two red cars and a blue lorry – and put them in a line (the traffic jam) snaking around under the tent.

5. Stand up carefully, lifting the parachute high in the air.

More ideas...

▶ Use soft toys with the parachute. Ask each child in turn to listen as you say "Put teddy and rabbit under the parachute", "Put the doll on the parachute", "Put the bear under the parachute", or even "Make teddy bounce across the parachute".

▶ Play a music tape and waft the parachute up and down to the music. Stop the music often and suddenly. When the music stops the children need to hold the parachute still.

Activity suitable for:

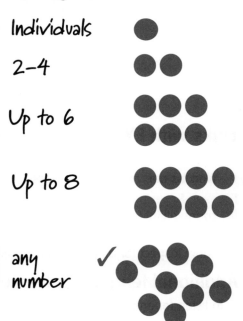

Individuals

2-4

Up to 6

Up to 8

any number

Look Out!

Focus: Use shape targets for a different listening game

What you need

I will need

▶ paper, paint and trays
▶ printing shapes
▶ masking tape
▶ bean bags

Links with EYFS goals

Problem Solving, Reasoning and Numeracy
▶ select a particular named shape

Physical Development
▶ persevere in repeating some actions/attempts
  when developing a new skill

Additional learning outcomes

– To listen for and act on a sound

– To recognise colours

– To stretch up high, bend down low and sit down
  at the same time as the group

Key words

▶ shape names
▶ close/far away
▶ watch
▶ listen
▶ aim
▶ throw

What you do

1. Cut some big paper shapes – choose simple shapes e.g. circle, triangle, square, oblong, star.

2. Print the paper shapes with shape printers (bricks, stamps, potato cuts, etc.). Try to use outline shapes as well. Match the print shape with the paper shape (circles on circle, etc.).

3. When dry, tape the shapes to the floor, indoors or outside.

4. Give each child a bean bag and let them practice throwing them on the shapes before doing the next part of the game.

5. Now take turns to throw a bean bag onto a named shape, when you click your fingers or clap. They must listen carefully for the signal before throwing.

6. Choose another shape and play again.

More ideas...

▶ Give each child two beanbags and let them run through the shapes dropping their beanbags on two named shapes.

▶ Play a silly animal sounds game. Use just three shapes and agree three different animal sounds, one to indicate each shape, such as a "baa" for the circle, a "moo" for the square and a "cluck" for the triangle. For younger children, you could stand a farmyard animal on each shape to help them remember.

Activity suitable for:

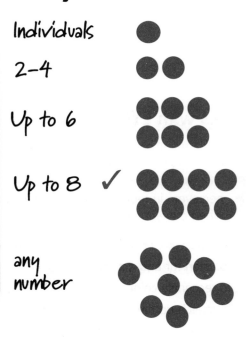

Individuals

2–4

Up to 6

Up to 8 ✓

any number

Pass the Sound!

Focus: **A circle game for listening and remembering**

What you need

- ▶ a tray
- ▶ four sound makers: e.g. drum, shaker,

wooden blocks, rainmaker, chime bar, keys, spoons and a box of cereal

I will need

Links with EYFS goals

Personal, Social and Emotional Development
- ▶ be confident to try new activities, and speak in a familiar group.

Communication, Language and Literacy
- ▶ use a widening range of words to express and elaborate ideas.

Additional learning outcomes

- – To describe sounds
- – To listen to and recall a series of sounds
- – To take turns

Key words

- ▶ high/low
- ▶ loud/soft
- ▶ same/different
- ▶ similar
- ▶ bang/tap
- ▶ rattle

What you do

1. Gather the children in a circle and put the tray of objects in the middle.

2. Pass the sound makers round and have a go with them. Talk about and describe the sounds.

3. Make two sounds – eg. the blocks and then the chime bar.

4. Slide the tray to the child next to you. Let them try to repeat the sounds in the same order. Prompt them with comments such as, "The first sound was a tapping sound."

5. Slide the tray on round the circle, so each child has a turn with the same sound pattern.

6. If they can repeat a pattern of two sounds, try three or four.

More ideas...

▶ Let each child choose a sound maker. Make a simple pattern for them to copy all together or in turns round the circle.

▶ Play the game with lots of wooden objects that make different sounds, such as different pieces of wood, bark, twigs, wooden boxes, wooden bricks, or wooden bricks in a wooden box and so on.

▶ Or play a metal sounds game with spoons, forks, tubes, tins, lids, strings of washers, etc.

Activity suitable for:

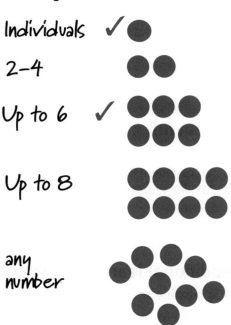

Individuals ✓

2-4

Up to 6 ✓

Up to 8

any number

Hop, Skip and Jump!

Focus: A simple listening game with big movements

What you need

▶ a large space
▶ a chime bar, triangle, tambourine or drum

I will need

Links with EYFS goals

Personal, Social and Emotional Development
▶ display high levels of involvement.

Communication, Language and Literacy
▶ sustain attentive listening.

Personal Development
▶ show awareness of space, of themselves and others.

Additional learning outcomes

– To follow simple rules
– To listen to signals for start and stop
– To follow simple rules

Key words

▶ backwards/forwards
▶ crawl/creep
▶ wiggle
▶ roll
▶ spin
▶ body words

What you do

1. Ask all the children to sit on the floor and then to stretch out their arms. If they can reach the child next to them they need to move and find a bigger space.

2. Explain that you are going to play a listening game and that the children will need to follow an instruction – when you sound the chime bar (or other instrument) twice this means "go", when they hear just one beat on the instrument it means "stop".

3. Start with a simple movement such as walking or running.

4. Now make the movements more complex, such as wriggling along on their tummy, hopping, giant strides, rolling, side steps. Always use the same cue for starting and stopping.

More ideas...

► Add some smaller movements such as clapping, rolling arms, tapping fingers and toes, touching elbows on knees and so on.

► Ask the children to move like different animals, toys or machines.

► Play a slow motion game where the actions are carried out incredibly slowly. When they hear a shaker sound, they start moving very quickly.

► Give children turns at choosing the actions and playing the instruments.

Activity suitable for:

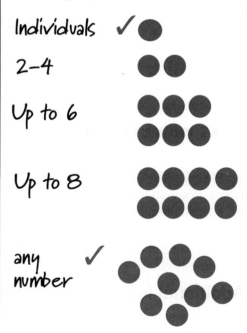

Individuals ✓

2-4

Up to 6

Up to 8

any number ✓

Roll it!

Focus: **Practice early ball skills and listening**

What you need

- footballs, beach balls, rubber or plastic balls, ping pong balls and tennis balls
- a large space

Links with EYFS goals

Personal, Social and Emotional Development
- work as part of a group or class taking turns and sharing fairly.

Communication, Language and Literacy
- speak clearly and audibly.
- use a range of small equipment.

Additional learning outcomes

- To recognise and say children's names
- To roll a ball gently in a specific direction
- To stop a rolling ball
- To take turns and follow rules

Key words

- ready, steady, go
- rolling
- stop
- fast/slow
- look
- listen

What you do

1. Gather the children in a circle and explain the game.

2. Demonstrate by calling a child's name and gently rolling a ball to them. They catch the ball and roll it back to you.

3. When they understand this bit, make the game more difficult by encouraging the children to send the ball to another child (they must say the name, and look at the child as they roll).

4. When they are ready, speed the game up so the ball is travelling between children much faster.

5. For older or more practised children try with two balls at once, going to different children! (This is much more difficult!)

More ideas...

▶ Use a simple sound maker to indicate when the ball should move on. This time, the children must just look at the next child before rolling the ball.

▶ Sing a song as you play e.g. "The ball in the ring goes rolling on, rolling on, rolling on..." to the tune of "The Wheels on the Bus".

▶ Play these games outside with a hoop or beach ball. Make the circle bigger for larger movements and even more listening skills!

Activity suitable for:

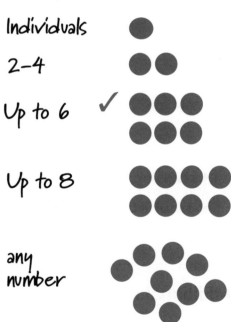

Individuals

2-4

Up to 6 ✓

Up to 8

any number

Sound Hunt

Focus: **A game for matching and sorting sounds**

What you need

▶ a big space outside

Links with EYFS goals

Personal, Social and Emotional Development
▶ demonstrate flexibility and adapt their behaviour to different events.

Communication, Language and Literacy
▶ show an awareness of rhyme and alliteration

Additional learning outcomes

– To distinguish between and identify sounds

– To continue a rhyming string

Key words

▶ click, clank

▶ ring, ting

▶ rustle

▶ crinkle

▶ pop, bang

▶ jingle

What you do

1. Take a walk around the garden or outside play area. Make sounds by stamping on different surfaces, brushing, rustling leaves, tapping metal, knocking on wooden fences, scraping leaves together, sprinkling sand, dripping water, etc.

2. Talk about the sounds and use words to describe them. Encourage rhyming words such as rustle and hustle, tap and clap, brush and hush.

3. Now make some outside music. Use the sounds you have made to make a sound pattern or accompany a song such as "Here we go Round the Mulberry Bush" - using "Here we go tapping on the tree..." "Here we go rustling in the leaves..." "Here we go stamping on the path..."

More ideas...

▶ Do some baking together and focus on the different sounds that you can hear or make, such as a wooden spoon tapping the mixing bowl, spoons clanking on tins or the water being poured.

▶ Ask the children to think about the sounds you may hear on a trip to the supermarket. Make a list of these together using words, pictures and symbols. Take a trip to the supermarket and tick off each sound you hear, and add new sounds to your list.

Activity suitable for:

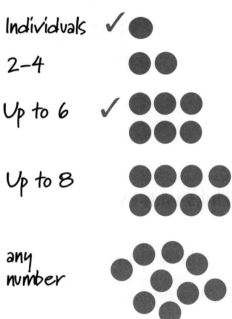

Individuals ✓

2-4

Up to 6 ✓

Up to 8

any number

Dress It Up!

Focus: **Listen and take turns with dressing up fun**

What you need

I will need

▶ a cassette recorder
▶ dressing up clothes
▶ shoes, bags and jewellery
▶ ties, cases and hats

Links with EYFS goals

Personal, Social and Emotional Development
▶ dress and undress independently.

Physical Development
▶ persevere in repeating some actions/attempts when developing a new skill

Additional learning outcomes

– To listen for information carrying words

– To manage simple fastenings

– To work together, offering help and support

Key words

▶ shiny, soft
▶ silky, smooth
▶ furry, bumpy
▶ warm, cool
▶ body words
▶ on/off

What you do

1. Pre-record some instructions for the children to follow, such as "Put on something for a sunny day", "Something shiny", "Something warm", "Something blue", "Something waterproof". Slip in some crazy requests, such as "Put a glove on your foot", or "Put on a dress back to front".

2. Look through the dressing up clothes and other items with the children. Talk about when you could wear them, what sort of material they are made of, their colours and textures.

3. Play the tape, pausing between each instruction. If there are plenty of dressing up clothes, each child can complete each instruction. Otherwise, they can take turns to follow an instruction. Look at the results in a mirror.

More ideas...

▶ Draw the outline of a person or a simple picture on a piece of paper, one for each child. Ask the children to listen to the tape and colour the right bit of the picture.

▶ Add other things to the box, such as gloves, wellies, swimwear, hats, armbands, and so on. The children work in pairs, taking turns to choose items for their partner to put on.

▶ Pre-record a list of dolls' clothes and accessories. Play this game, using dolls, teddies or soft toys.

Activity suitable for:

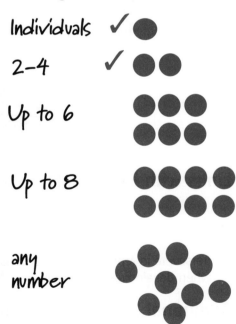

Individuals ✓

2–4 ✓

Up to 6

Up to 8

any number

Book List

Here are some stories that are particularly useful in encouraging attentive listening, concentration and awareness of rhythm and rhyme:

The Bear Hunt

Mrs Wishy Washy

Don't Forget the Bacon

Pass the Jam, Jim

You Can Swim Jim

Need a Trim, Jim?

The Cat in The Hat

Green Eggs and Ham

Mrs Brown Can Moo, Can You?

Mrs Mopple's Washing Line

Brown Bear, Brown Bear What do You See?

The Shopping Basket

Rosie's Walk

The Gruffalo

I've Lost My Mum